TO YOUR SUCCESS

THOUGHTS TO GIVE WINGS TO YOUR WORK AND YOUR DREAMS

COMPILED BY
DAN ZADRA

DESIGNED BY
KOBI YAMADA AND STEVE POTTER

COMPENDIUM™
PUBLISHING

live inspired.

ACKNOWLEDGEMENTS
These quotations were gathered lovingly but unscientifically over several years and or contributed by many friends or acquaintances. Some arrived—and survived in our files—on scraps of paper and may therefore be imperfectly worded or attributed. To the authors, contributors and original sources, our thanks, and where appropriate, our apologies. —The editors

WITH SPECIAL THANKS TO
Jason Aldrich, Gerry Baird, Jay Baird, Neil Beaton, Doug Cruickshank, Jim Darragh, Jennifer & Matt Ellison, Josie & Rob Estes, Michael Flynn, Jennifer Hurwitz, Liam Lavery, Connie McMartin, Cristal & Brad Olberg, Janet Potter & Family, Aimee Rawlins, Diane Roger, Drew Wilkie, Jenica Wilkie, Robert & Mary Anne Wilkie, Heidi & Shale Yamada, Justi, Tote & Caden Yamada, Robert & Val Yamada, Kaz, Kristin, Kyle & Kendyl Yamada, Tai & Joy Yamada, Anne Zadra, August & Arline Zadra and Dan Zadra.

CREDITS
Compiled by Dan Zadra
Designed by Kobi Yamada & Steve Potter

Printed in Hong Kong

CONTENTS

DREAM
Hopes, Dreams and Possibilities
Visions, Goals and Plans
Imagination, Creativity and Innovation

6

TEAM
Collaboration, Teamwork and Leadership
Loyalty, Synergy, and Friendship
Communication, Cooperation and Coordination

36

CARE
Pride, Passion and Commitment
Quality, Integrity and Service
Values, Expectations and Standards

66

DARE
Confidence, Courage and Tenacity
Choices, Decisions, and Action
Freedom, Opportunity and Fulfillment

96

A GIFT TO INSPIRE AND CELEBRATE YOUR ACHIEVEMENTS

Chances are you received this little book from someone who believes in you or appreciates what you do.

"I believe in you. I appreciate what you do. Here's to your success." Sincerely offered by the right person at the right time, the simplest words can often mean the most to us.

Take these words: dream, team, care, dare. Or these: integrity, craftsmanship, quality, responsibility, courage, faith, imagination, tenacity. If you place a high value on these simple terms, you will find—as I have—that the men and women quoted in this book are kindred spirits.

Compiling these great quotations for you has been a terrific experience. I realized once again that some of the most powerful, timeless and useful ideas are also the shortest. "God bless America" is just three words, but three are all that's required. Shakespeare's "To thine own self be true" is just six words, but those six could make a life. The Lord's Prayer has 71 words; the Gettysburg Address has 271; the Ten Commandments have 297; the marriage vow just two.

The thoughts in this book average fewer than 35 words, and each is sincerely dedicated to your success. May this book become a source of inspiration and joy for you—just as your own work, dreams and accomplishments are an inspiration to others.

Dan Zadra

For my hero, Augie Zadra

IF YOU

CAN DREAM IT,

YOU CAN DO IT.

—WALT DISNEY

DREAM

EVERY CANDLE EVER LIT; EVERY HOME, BRIDGE, CATHEDRAL OR CITY EVER BUILT; EVERY ACT OF HUMAN KINDNESS, DISCOVERY, DARING, ARTISTRY OR ADVANCE-MENT STARTED FIRST IN SOME-ONE'S IMAGINATION, AND THEN WORKED ITS WAY OUT. YOU HAVE THAT POWER—USE IT.

If you do not
think about the future,
you cannot have one.

—JOHN GALE

If you don't have a dream, how can
you have a dream come true?

—FAYE LAPOINTE

Your past is not your potential.
In any hour you can choose
to liberate the future.

—MARILYN FERGUSON

If you keep doing
what you've always done,
you'll keep getting
what you've always got.

–PETER FRANCISCO

Man is the only animal that laughs
and weeps, for he is the only animal
that is struck with the difference
between what things are, and
what they ought to be.

–WILLIAM HAZLITT

Dreams come a size too big
so that we can grow into them.

–JOSIE BISSETT

10

Far away there in the sunshine
are my highest aspirations. I may not
reach them, but I can look up and see
their beauty, believe in them, and try
to follow where they lead.

–LOUISA MAY ALCOTT

I like the dreams of the future
better than the history of the past.

–THOMAS JEFFERSON

To look up with unquenchable faith
in something evermore about to be.
That is what any person can do,
and be great.

–ZANE GREY

Humanity cannot forget its dreamers;
it cannot let their ideals fade and die;
it knows them as the realities which
it shall one day see and know.

—JAMES ALLEN

12

My interest is in
the future, because I am going to
spend the rest of my life there.

—CHARLES F. KETTERING

The greatest achievement
was at first and for a time a dream.
The oak sleeps in the acorn;
the bird waits in the egg; and in the highest
vision of the soul a waking angel stirs.

—WILLIAM JAMES

13

Your hopes, dreams and
aspirations are legitimate. They are trying
to take you airborne, above the clouds, above
the storms—if you will only let them.

—DAN ZADRA

Life is a series of collisions
with the future; it is not the sum
of what we have been, but what
we yearn to be.

–JOSE ORTEGA Y GASSET

14

When one door closes, another opens;
but we often look so long and
so regretfully upon the closed door
that we do not see the one
which has opened for us.

–ALEXANDER GRAHAM BELL

Lord, grant that I may always
desire more than I can accomplish.

—MICHELANGELO

When dreams die, life is a
broken-winged bird that cannot fly.

—LANGSTON HUGHES

When you're through changing,
you're through.

—BRUCE BARTON

15

I had no ambition to make a fortune.
Mere money-making has never been my goal.
I had an ambition to build.

—JOHN D. ROCKEFELLER

16

Some men march to the beat
of a different drummer, and some polka.

—ANONYMOUS

Two men look through the self-same bars;
one sees mud, and one sees the stars.

—FREDERICK LANGBRIDGE

Dreams are renewable.
No matter what your age or condition,
there are still untapped possibilities
within you and new beauty
waiting to be born.

—DR. DALE E. TURNER

17

The greatest thing in this world
is not so much where we stand, as in
what direction we are moving.

—GOETHE

Extraordinary people visualize not
what is possible or probable, but rather what is
impossible. And by visualizing the impossible,
they begin to see it as possible.

–CHERIE CARTER-SCOTT

18

Some men see things as they are
and ask, "why?" I dream things that
never were and ask, "why not?"

–GEORGE BERNARD SHAW

Set your sights high, the higher the better.
Expect the most wonderful things to happen,
not in the future, but right now.
Realize that nothing is too good.

—EILEEN CADDY

When we set exciting worthwhile goals
for ourselves, they work in two ways:
We work on them, and they work on us.

—EDGE LEARNING

Keep a daily diary of your
dreams, goals and accomplishments.
If your life is worth living,
it's worth recording.

—MARILYN GREY

20

Written goals have a way of transforming
wishes into wants; can'ts into cans;
dreams into plans; and plans into reality.
Don't just think it—ink it!

—DAN ZADRA

Don't pray for dreams equal
to your powers. Pray for powers
equal to your dreams.

–MICHAEL NOLAN

Your imagination can focus on
ugliness, distress and failure, or it can
picture beauty, success, desired results.
You decide how you want your
imagination to serve you.

–PHILIP CONLEY

21

If we wish to make
a new world, we have the
material handy. The first one, too,
was made out of chaos.

–ROBERT QUILLEN

22

You do not need to know how you're
actually going to achieve a goal when
you set it. Just repeatedly visualize
the desired result, and the
"how" will open up to you.

–VINCE PFAFF

DREAM

Dream lofty dreams,
and as you dream, so shall
you become. Your vision is the
promise of what you shall
one day be.

—JAMES ALLEN

23

The future is of our own making—and
the most striking characteristic of this
century is just that development.

—JOSEPH CONRAD

The first and most important thing
about goals is having one.

—GEOFFREY ABERT

The future never just happened.
It was created.

—WILL & ARIEL DURANT

You cannot take charge of the present
if you are busy reliving the
setbacks of the past.

—NEWMAN & BERKOWITZ

24

Great minds have purposes;
others have wishes.

–WASHINGTON IRVING

If you built castles in the air,
your work need not be lost;
that is where they should be.
Now put foundations
under them.

–HENRY DAVID THOREAU

25

Those who dream by night wake to find
that it was vanity. But the dreamers of day
are dangerous; they may act out their dreams
with open eyes to make it possible.

–T.E. LAWRENCE

26

You have brains in your head,
and feet in your shoes. You can steer
yourself any direction you choose.

–DR. SEUSS

Reach beyond your grasp.
Your goals should be grand enough
to get the best of you.

–TEILHARD DE CHARDIN

27

Throughout the centuries
there were men who took first steps
down new roads armed with nothing
but their own vision.

–AYN RAND

Genius seems to be the faculty
of having faith in everything,
especially oneself.

—ARTHUR STRINGER

Imagination is the beginning of creation.
We imagine what we desire;
we will what we imagine;
and at last we create what we will.

—GEORGE BERNARD SHAW

A genius is a person
who aims at something no one else
can see and hits it.

—ERVIN L. GLASPY

I shut my eyes in order to see.

—PAUL GAUGUIN

The innovator is not an opponent
of the old, he is a proponent
of the new.

—LYLE E. SCHALLER

Discovery is seeing what
everybody else has seen, and thinking
what nobody else has thought.

—ALBERT SZENT-GYORGI

30

Take out your brain and jump on it—
it gets all caked up.

—MARK TWAIN

To stay ahead, you must have your
next idea waiting in the wings.

—ROSABETH MOSS KANTER

Choose to live, work and succeed
in the most powerful nation on earth:
Imagination.

—DAN ZADRA

Imagination is more important
than knowledge.

—ALBERT EINSTEIN

Often you just have to rely on your intuition.

—BILL GATES, MICROSOFT

Just think of something that everyone
agrees would be "wonderful" if it were only
"possible." Then set out to make it possible.

—ARMAND HAMMER

A No. 2 pencil and a dream
can take you anywhere.

—J. MEYERS

Keep one still, secret spot where dreams may go
and, sheltered so, may thrive and grow.

—CHILDREN'S RHYME

32

Sorrow looks back.
Worry looks around. Faith looks ahead.

–BEATRICE FALLON

You can't help getting older, but
you don't have to get old. New dreams,
new works in progress—that's the ticket
for a long and happy ride.

–GEORGE BURNS

Never fear the space between your dreams
and reality. If you can dream it,
you can make it so.

–BELVA DAVIS

DREAM

Every thought is a seed.
If you plant crab apples, don't count
on harvesting Golden Delicious.

—BILL MEYER

To make a prairie
it takes a clover and one bee.
One clover, and a bee, and reverie.
And reverie alone will do,
if bees are few.

—EMILY DICKINSON

Money never starts an idea;
it is the idea that starts the money.

–W.J. CAMERON

Whatever you're ready for is ready for you.

–MARK VICTOR HANSEN

Hats off to the past.
Coats off to the future!

–AMERICAN PROVERB

NO MATTER
WHAT GREAT THINGS
YOU ACCOMPLISH
SOMEBODY
HELPS YOU.

—WILMA RUDOLPH

TEAM

NO ONE GOES ALONE TO THE HEIGHTS OF EXCELLENCE. WHETHER YOUR BUSINESS IS BUILDING A LOVING FAMILY, A GREAT IDEA, A MEANINGFUL CAREER, A WORK OF ART, OR A VAST COMMERCIAL EMPIRE, YOUR SUCCESS WILL DEPEND ON OTHERS, AND THEIRS WILL DEPEND ON YOU.

You can dream, create,
design, and build the most wonderful
idea in the world, but it requires people
to make the dream a reality.

—WALT DISNEY

38

Anything one person can imagine,
other people can make real.

—JULES VERNE

Americans will reach the moon
by standing on each other's shoulders.

–JOHN F. KENNEDY

No one can whistle a symphony.
It takes an orchestra to play it.

–H.E. LUCCOCK

39

Problems can become opportunities when
the right people come together.

–ROBERT REDFORD

TEAM

None of us is as smart as all of us.

–KEN BLANCHARD

Winners can tell you where they are going,
what they plan to do along the way and who will
be sharing the adventure with them.

–DENIS WAITLEY

Working together works.

–DR. ROB GILBERT

40

Every great pitcher needs a great catcher.

–CASEY STENGEL

Search for eagles and then teach
them to fly in formation.

–D. WAYNE CALLOWAY

There is greatness all around you—
welcome it! It is easy to be great when
you get around great people.

–BOB RICHARDS

We have to be able to
count on each other doing what
we have agreed to do.

–PHIL CROSBY

42

You can work miracles by having
faith in others. To get the best out
of people, choose to think and
believe the best about them.

–BOB MOAWAD

Nothing binds us one to the other
like a promise kept. Nothing divides us
like a promise broken.

—MASS MUTUAL

To promote cooperation and teamwork,
remember: People tend to resist that which is
forced upon them. People tend to support that
which they help to create.

—VINCE PFAFF

Ask your team—they know the answer.

—CHUCK CARLSON

Never kill an idea, just deflect it.

—3M SLOGAN

This is a team effort. If you can't
put people up, please don't put them down.

—NASA SLOGAN

44

I'm just a country plowhand,
but I've learned to get a team beating with
one heart: If anything goes bad, I did it.
If anything goes semi-good, we did it.
If anything goes real good, they did it.

–PAUL "BEAR" BRYANT

45

The best leaders are very often
the best listeners. They have an open mind.
They are not interested in having their own way
but in finding the best way.

–WILFRED PETERSON

Either we're pulling together,
or we're pulling apart.
There's really no in-between.

–B.J. MARSHALL

If you're too busy to help those
around you succeed, you're too busy.

–BOB MOAWAD

The best minute you spend
is the one you invest in people.

–BLANCHARD & JOHNSON

Motivation is everything.
You can do the work of two people,
but you can't be two people. Instead,
you have to inspire the next guy down
the line to get him to inspire his people.

–LEE IACOCCA

There is a place for everyone in the
big picture. To turn your back on any one
person, for whatever reason, is to run
the risk of losing the central piece
of your jigsaw puzzle.

–JAMES ST. LYON

It's a fine thing to have ability,
but the ability to discover ability in others
is the true test.

—ELBERT HUBBARD

There is no exercise better for the heart
than reaching down and lifting people up.

—JOHN A. HOLMES

Those who are lifting the world
upward and onward are those who
encourage more than criticize.

—ELIZABETH HARRISON

48

If he works for you, you work for him.
–JAPANESE PROVERB

Leave no one out of the big picture.
Involve everyone in everything of any
consequence to all of you.
–TOM PETERS

March in right now and clear the air.
–UNITED TECHNOLOGIES

Help each other be right,
not wrong. Look for ways to make
new ideas work, not for reasons they won't.
Do everything with enthusiasm,
it's contagious.

—IAN PERCY

50

Trust each other again and again.
When the trust level gets high enough,
people transcend apparent limits, discovering
new and awesome abilities for which
they were previously unaware.

—DAVID ARMISTEAD

Leadership is action, not position.

–DONALD H. MCGANNON

There are no passengers on Spaceship Earth.
Everybody's crew.

–MARSHALL MCLUHAN

There is something that is much more scarce,
something rarer than ability. It is the
ability to recognize ability.

–ROBERT HALF

Teamwork is
less "ego" and more "we go."

–BRIAN BIRO

52

The great companies and teams
are those that celebrate the differences.
They seek harmony not uniformity.
They hire talent not color. They strive
for oneness not sameness.

–GIL ATKINSON

A team can win with almost any offense,
provided everyone on the team
is playing the same offense.

–JOHN WOODEN

Mountain climbers always help each other.

–TENZING NORGAY, SHERPA

The best thing to
hold onto in life is each other.

–AUDREY HEPBURN

If you want help, help others.
If you want trust, trust others. If you
want love, give it away. If you want friends,
be one. If you want a great team, be a
great teammate. That's how it works.

—DAN ZADRA

54

Life and business are like the
carpool lane. The best way to reach
your destination quickly is to
take some people with you.

—PETE WARD

Excellence is what you and
your people create on your turf.
It can be done and it is done. There is
no excuse for not getting on with it
among your people.

—TOM PETERS

There are two ways of exerting
one's strength—one is pushing down,
and the other is pulling up.

—BOOKER T. WASHINGTON

Most of us, swimming against the
tides of troubles the world knows
nothing about, need only a bit
of praise or encouragement—
and we'll make the goal.

—J.P. FLEISHMAN

56

We could all take a lesson from
the Great Northern Geese which fly
thousands of miles in perfect formation.
Formation flying is 70 percent more
efficient than flying alone.

—DAN ZADRA

Great discoveries and achievements
invariably involve the cooperation
of many minds.

—ALEXANDER GRAHAM BELL

Progress is 95 percent routine
teamwork. The other 5 percent relies
on restless, inner-directed people who
are willing to upset our apple cart
with new and better ideas.

—MICHAEL LEBOEUF

57

The secret is to
work less as individuals and
more as a team. As a coach,
I play not my eleven best,
but my best eleven.

–KNUTE ROCKNE

58

Where all think alike,
no one thinks very much.

–WALTER LIPPMANN

It is not fair to ask of others
what you are not willing to do yourself.

–ELEANOR ROOSEVELT

One step by 100 persons
is better than 100 steps by one person.

–KOICHI TSUKAMOTO

Remember the law
of accumulation: The sum
of many little collaborative
efforts isn't little.

–MICHAEL NOLAN

TEAM

Give all the credit away.

–JOHN WOODEN

The main ingredient
in stardom is the rest of the team.

–JOHN WOODEN

The only sacred cow
in an organization is its principles.

–BUCK RODGERS, IBM

The greatest thing you can do
for any individual or any group in your
day is to help them find the best.

–KATHERINE LOGAN

The real winners in life are the
people who look at every situtation
with an expectation that they can
make it work or make it better.

–BARBARA PLETCHER

Do good things for others and people
may accuse you of selfish motives.
Do good anyway.

–MOTHER TERESA

Don't over-react to the trouble makers.

–WARREN BENNIS

There are no exceptions
to the rule that everybody likes
to be an exception to the rule.

–MALCOLM FORBES

62

It's easier for people to see it
your way if you first see it their way.

–JACK KAINE

We must learn to lift as we climb.

–ANGELA DAVIS

The two kinds of people
on earth that I mean,
Are the people who lift and
the people who lean.

–ELLA WHEELER WILCOX

Any manager who can't
get along with a .400 hitter is crazy.

–JOE MCCARTHY

In the heroic organizations,
people mentor each other unselfishly.

–DON GALER

The best team doesn't win nearly
as often as the team that
gets along best.

–DR. ROB GILBERT

Celebrate what you want to see more of.

–TOM PETERS

Could a greater miracle take place
than for us to look through each other's
eyes for an instant?

–HENRY DAVID THOREAU

Be kind to one another.

–JIM HENSON, SESAME STREET

GIVE THE WOLRD
THE BEST THAT
YOU HAVE, AND
THE BEST WILL COME
BACK TO YOU.

—MADELINE BRIDGES

CARE

NO CALLING ON EARTH IS INSIG-NIFICANT IF IT IS ACCOMPLISHED WITH PRIDE AND ARTISTRY. DO WHATEVER YOUR HEART LEADS YOU TO DO, BUT DO IT SO WELL THAT THOSE WHO COME TO SEE YOU DO IT WILL BRING OTHERS TO WATCH YOU DO IT AGAIN AND AGAIN AND AGAIN.

If you love what you do,
you will never work another day in your life.

–CONFUCIOUS

The more you love what you are doing,
the more successful it will be for you.

–JERRY GILLIES

To love what you do and feel that it matters—
how could anything be more fun?

–KATHARINE GRAHAM

68

If you are working on something
exciting that you really care about, you don't
have to be pushed. The vision pulls you.

—STEPHEN JOBS

There's no grander sight in the world than
that of a person fired with a great purpose,
dominated by one unwavering aim.

—ORISON SWETT MARDEN

69

To make a living is no longer enough.
Work also has to make a life.

—PETER DRUCKER

He who has a 'why'
to live for can bear almost any 'how.'

–NIETZSCHE

Good work is never done in cold blood;
heat is needed to forge anything. Every great
achievement is the story of a flaming heart.

–A.C. CARLSON

If a man hasn't discovered something
that he will die for, he isn't fit to live.

–MARTIN LUTHER KING, JR.

CARE.

Care enough for a result,
and you will almost certainly attain it.

–WILLIAM JAMES

Never let what you
cannot do interfere with what you can do.

–JOHN WOODEN

Talent is what you possess;
genius is what possesses you.

–MALCOLM CROWLEY

Life is no brief candle to me.
It is a sort of splendid torch which I have
got hold of for the moment, and I want
to make it burn as brightly as possible
before handing it on to future generations.

–GEORGE BERNARD SHAW

72

Live your life so that your children
can tell their children that you not only
stood for something wonderful—
you acted on it.

–DAN ZADRA

Nobody grows old merely by living
a number of years. We grow old by
deserting our ideals. Years may wrinkle
the skin, but to give up enthusiasm
wrinkles the soul.

–SAMUEL ULLMAN

73

When we do the best we can,
we never know what miracle is wrought
in our life, or in the life of another.

–HELEN KELLER

Don't care what others think
of what you do; but care very much
about what you think you do.

–ST. FRANCES DE SALES

74

Life owes us little; we owe
it everything. The only true happiness
comes from squandering ourselves
for a purpose.

–JOHN MARM BROWN

Integrity is what we do,
what we say, and what we say we do.

—DON GALER

People don't really care
how much you know until they know
how much you care.

—MIKE MCNIGHT

There is no such thing
as a minor lapse of integrity.

—TOM PETERS

One person can make a difference
and every person should try.

–JOHN F. KENNEDY

The lure of the distant and the
difficult is deceptive. The great
opportunity is where you are.

–JOHN BURROUGHS

The place you are in
needs you today.

–KATHARINE LOGAN

Good ideas are not adopted
automatically. They must be driven into
practice with courageous patience.

—ADMIRAL HYMAN RICKOVER

77

Some succeed because they are
destined to; most succeed because
they are determined to.

—ANATOLE FRANCE

CARE

Act as if what you do
makes a difference. It does.

–WILLIAM JAMES

Let me tell you the secret that has
led me to my goal. My strength lies
solely in my tenacity.

–LOUIS PASTEUR

There is no failure
except in no longer trying.

–ELBERT HUBBARD

78

Most people never run
far enough on their first wind to find out
they've got a second. Give your dreams all
you've got and you'll be amazed at the energy
that comes out of you.

–WILLIAM JAMES

79

Tonight, when you lay your head
on your pillow, forget how far you still
have to go. Look instead at how far
you've already come.

–BOB MOAWAD

It's a funny thing about life.
If you refuse to accept anything
but the best, you very often get it.

–SOMERSET MAUGHAM

When you get right down
to the root of the meaning
of the word "succeed," you find
it simply means to follow through.

–F.W. NICHOL

Do what you can,
with what you have, where you are.

−THEODORE ROOSEVELT

One person with a belief is equal
to a force of ninety-nine who have
only interests.

−JOHN STUART HILL

There is no traffic jam on the extra mile.

−BUSINESS AXIOM

God will not look you over
for medals, degrees or diplomas,
but for scars.

—ELBERT HUBBARD

82

There is no finish line.

—NIKE MOTTO

Those who stand
for nothing may fall for anything.

—ALEXANDER HAMILTON

It's easy to have faith in yourself when
you're a winner, when you're number one.
What you've got to have is faith in yourself
when you're not a winner.

–VINCE LOMBARDI

Progress results only from the fact
that there are some men and women
who refuse to believe that what
they know to be right cannot be done.

–RUSSELL DAVENPORT

Anybody can come up with new ideas.
What's in short supply are innovative people—
persistent mavericks who believe so strongly
in an idea, they will do whatever it takes
to make it a working reality.

–MICHAEL LEBOEUF

84

It's important to take pride in what you do
or what you stand for. The kind of pride
I'm talking about is not the arrogant
puffed-up kind; it's just the whole idea
of caring—fiercely caring.

–RED AURBACH

Enthusiasm is contagious.
Start an epidemic.

–DON WARD

The best part of one's life
is the working part, the creative part.
Believe me, I love to succeed; but
the real spiritual and emotional
excitement is in the doing.

–GARSON KANIN

You can outdo you–if you really want to.

–PAUL HARVEY

Age puzzles me. I thought it was
a quiet time. My seventies were interesting and
fairly serene, but my eighties are passionate.
I grow more intense as I age.

–FLORIDA SCOTT-MAXWELL

86

The fight is won or lost far away
from witnesses—behind the lines, in the gym
and out there on the road, long before
I dance under those lights.

–MUHAMMAD ALI

As you get older, don't slow down.
Speed up. There's less time left.

−MALCOLM FORBES

It's what we learn
after we know it all that counts.

−A.C. CARLSON

Throw your heart over the bars
and your body will follow.

−VETERAN TRAPEZE PERFORMER

I must not rust.

–CLARA BARTON

Which of you is going to step up
and put me out to pasture?

–JOHN WAYNE

You may occasionally
give out—but never give up.

–MARY CROWLEY

88

Blessed are those
who expect nothing, for they
shall not be disappointed.

–JONATHAN SWIFT

Quality never goes out of style.

–LEVI STRAUSS

School is never out for the pro.

–JIM WILLIAMSON

Good enough never is.

–DEBBI FIELDS

In communities where
men build ships for their own
sons to fish or fight from,
quality is never a problem.

–J. DEVILLE

When your heart is in your dream,
no request is too extreme.

–JIMINY CRICKET

People don't give a hoot
about who made the original whatzit.
They want to know who makes
the best one.

–HOWARD W. NEWTON

The greatest crime in the world
is not developing your potential.
When you do what you do best,
you are helping others.

–ROGER WILLIAMS

The road to success has
many tempting parking places.

–STEVE POTTER

The winds blow strongest
against those who stand tallest.

–F.C. HAYES

Prepare. The time to win your
battle is before it starts.

–FREDERICK W. LEWIS

92

Quitting is a permanent solution
to a temporary situation.

–DR. ROB GILBERT

Success requires three bones—
wishbone, backbone and funnybone.

–KOBI YAMADA

Take your job seriously
but learn to laugh at yourself.

–DON WARD

93

Enthusiasm is faith set on fire.

–GEORGE ADAMS

Formula for success:
Underpromise and overdeliver.

–TOM PETERS

When the one Great Scorer comes
to write against your name, He marks—
not that you won or lost—but how
you played the game.

–GRANTLAND RICE

If you consistently do your best,
the worst will never happen.

–B.C. FORBES

Luck is earned. Luck is working
so hard at your craft, service or enterprise
that sooner or later you get a break.

–PAUL HAWKEN

The real friend of his country is the person
who believes in excellence, seeks for it, fights
for it, defends it, and tries to produce it.

–MORLEY CALLAGHAN

OUR FEARS
MUST NEVER
HOLD US BACK
FROM PURSUING
OUR HOPES.

—JOHN F. KENNEDY

DARE

THERE HAS BEEN A CALCULATED RISK IN EVERY STAGE OF AMERICAN DEVELOPMENT—PIONEERS WHO WERE UNAFRAID OF THE WILDERNESS, SCIENTISTS WHO WERE UNAFRAID OF THE TRUTH, BUSINESSMEN WHO WERE UNAFRAID OF FAILURE, DREAMERS WHO WERE UNAFRAID OF ACTION.

A great pleasure in life
is doing what people say you cannot do.

—WALTER GAGEHOT

Anything I've ever done that ultimately
was worthwhile…initially scared me to death.

—BETTY BENDER

The first and great
commandment is, never let them scare you.

—ELMER DAVIS

Take a chance!
All life is a chance. The person who
goes farthest is generally the one who is
willing to do and dare. The "sure thing"
boat never gets far from shore.

—DALE CARNEGIE

99

Take risks.
You can't fall off the bottom.

—BARBARA PROCTOR

The moment you commit and quit
holding back, all sorts of unforeseen incidents,
meetings and material assistance will rise up to
help you. The simple act of commitment is a
powerful magnet for help.

–NAPOLEON HILL

You can either take action,
or you can hang back and hope for
a miracle. Miracles are great, but they
are so unpredictable.

–PETER DRUCKER

People will try to tell you that all the great opportunities have been snapped up. In reality, the world changes every second, blowing new opportunities in all directions, including yours.

–KEN HAKUTA

To get profit without risk, experience without danger, and reward without work, is as impossible as it is to live without being born.

–A.P. GOUTHEY

Anyone with a new idea
is a crank—until the idea succeeds.

—MARK TWAIN

The biggest things are often
the easiest to do because there is
so little competition.

—WILLIAM VAN HORNE

Wherever you see a successful
business, someone once made
a courageous decision.

—PETER DRUCKER

It's a good idea
not to major in minor things.

–ANTHONY ROBBINS

Some things arrive in their own
mysterious hour, on their own terms and not
yours, to be seized or relinquished forever.

–GAIL GODWIN

The Wright Brothers flew right through the
smoke screen of impossibility.

–CHARLES F. KETTERING

All the beautiful sentiments in the
world weigh less than a single lovely action.

—JAMES RUSSELL LOWELL

Only begin and then the mind grows heated;
only begin and the task will be completed.

—GOETHE

Our duty is to proceed
as if limits to our ability do not exist.

—TEILHARD DE CHARDIN

Alas, for those who never sing,
but die with all their music in them.

–OLIVER WENDALL HOLMES, JR.

No, you never get any fun
out of the things you haven't done.

–OGDEN NASH

People who never
get carried away should be.

–MALCOLM FORBES

All humanity is divided
into three classes: those who
are immovable, those who
are movable and those who move!

—BENJAMIN FRANKLIN

106

Life is like a tiger. You can either
lie down and let it lay its paw
on your head—or you can
sit on its back and ride it.

—RIDE THE WILD TIGER

Argue for your limitations
and, sure enough, they're yours.

—RICHARD BACH

Do the thing and you will have the power.

—EMERSON

Others can stop you temporarily;
only you can do it permanently.

—DON WARD

As you grow older,
you'll find the only things you regret
are the things you didn't do.

–ZACHARY SCOTT

108

Sit, walk or run, but don't wobble.

–ZEN

Trust your crazy ideas.

–DAN ZADRA

I cannot give you
the formula for success, but
I can give you the formula for failure—
which is: Try to please everybody.

–H.B. SWOPE

109

Pay no attention to what
the critics say; no statue
has ever been erected to a critic.

–JEAN SIBELIUS

A good plan vigorously executed
right now is far better than a perfect
plan executed next week.

–GENERAL GEORGE PATTON

There are risks and costs to a
program of action—but they are far less
than the long-range risks and costs
of comfortable inaction.

–JOHN F. KENNEDY

Action is eloquence.

–SHAKESPEARE

Build it and they will come!

–FIELD OF DREAMS

If we did all the things
we are capable of, we would
literally astound ourselves.

–THOMAS EDISON

Our doubts are traitors, and
make us lose the good we oft might
win by fearing the attempt.

–SHAKESPEARE

Two roads diverged in a wood, and I—
I took the one less travelled by,
and that has made all the difference.

–ROBERT FROST

Don't be afraid to take a big step
if one is indicated. You can't cross
a chasm in two small jumps.

–DAVID LLOYD GEORGE

113

It is not because things are difficult
that we do not dare; it is because
we do not dare that things are difficult.

–SENECA

For every obstacle
there is a solution—over,
under, around or through.

—DAN ZADRA

Pick battles big enough
to matter, small enough to win.

—JONATHAN KOZOL

You have to think anyway,
so why not think big?

—DONALD TRUMP

Form the habit of saying
"Yes" to a good idea. Then write down
all the reasons why it will work. There will
always be plenty of people around you
to tell you why it won't work.

–GIL ATKINSON

You know far more than
you know you know. Never ask,
"Can I do this?" Ask instead,
"How can I do this?"

–DAN ZADRA

Chances are, the more puzzled looks
your idea creates, the better your idea is.

–UNITED TECHNOLOGIES

Live all you can; it's a mistake not to.

–HENRY JAMES

Use the word "impossible"
with the greatest caution.

–WERNER VON BRAUN

116

High achievers spot rich opportunities
swiftly, make big decisions quickly, and move
into action immediately. Follow these principles
and you can make your dreams come true.

–DR. ROBERT SCHULLER

You can't leave footprints in the
sands of time if you're sitting on your butt.
And who wants to leave buttprints
in the sands of time?

–BOB MOAWAD

Cause something to happen.

−PAUL "BEAR" BRYANT

It's amazing what ordinary people can do
if they set out without preconceived notions.

−CHARLES F. KETTERING

You can't build a reputation
on things you are going to do.

−HENRY FORD

I believe that genius is an
infinite capacity for taking life
by the scruff of the neck.

–CHRISTOPHER QUILL

The world is an oyster, but
you don't crack it open on a mattress.

–ARTHUR MILLER

There is only one you.
God wanted you to be you. Don't you dare
change just because you're outnumbered!

–CHARLES SWINDOLL

Anything is possible.
Nothing is too good to be true.

–KOBI YAMADA

Nothing splendid has ever
been achieved except by those who dared
believe that something inside them was
superior to circumstances.

–BRUCE BARTON

A year from now you may wish
you had started today.

–KAREN LAMB

All things come to those who go after them.

–B.J. MARSHALL

Let us go, now, and wake up our luck.

–PERSIAN PROVERB

Don't bunt. Aim out of the ballpark.

–DAVID OGILVIE

There is no security on this earth.
Only opportunity.

–DOUGLAS MACARTHUR

Why go into something to test the waters?
Go into it to make waves.

–MICHAEL NOLAN

Whenever the human adventure
reaches great and complete expression,
we can be sure it is because someone has
dared to be his unaverage self.

–RAE NOEL

You are one of a kind; therefore,
no one can really predict to what heights
you might soar. Even you will not know
until you spread your wings!

–GIL ATKINSON

If you risk nothing,
then you risk everything.

–GEENA DAVIS

124

The future is not a gift, it is an achievement.

–HENRY LAUDER

If you're already walking
on thin ice, you might as well dance.

–GIL ATKINSON

We must have courage to bet
on our ideas, to take the calculated risk,
and to act. Everyday living requires courage
if life is to be effective and bring happiness.

–MAXWELL MALTZ

And will you succeed?
Yes indeed, yes indeed! Ninety-eight
and three-quarters percent guaranteed!

–DR. SEUSS

The only safe ship in a storm
is leadership.

–FAYE WATTLETON

Never let anyone monkey with your swing.

–MICKEY MANTLE

Amateurs hope.
Professionals make it happen.

–GARSON KANIN

No matter what the statistics say,
there's always a way.

–BERNARD SIEGEL

Never mistake motion for action.

–ERNEST HEMINGWAY

There can be no progress unless
people have faith in tomorrow.

–JOHN F. KENNEDY

Also available from The Gift of Inspiration Series.

Be Happy.
Remember to Live, Love,
Laugh and Learn

Because of You™
Celebrating the Difference
You Make™

Be the Difference

Brilliance
Uncommon Voices From
Uncommon Women

Commitment to Excellence™
Celebrating the Very Best

Everyone Leads™
It takes each of us to make a
difference for all of us™

Expect Success

Forever Remembered™
A Gift for the Grieving Heart™

I Believe in You™
To your heart, your dream and
the difference you make

Little Miracles™
To renew your dreams,
lift your spirits, and strengthen
your resolve™

Reach for the Stars™
Give up the Good to Go
for the Great

Thank You
In appreciation of you,
and all that you do.

Together We Can™
Celebrating the power of
a team and a dream™

You've Got a Friend
Thoughts to Celebrate
the Joy of Friendship

Whatever It Takes
A Gift to inspire and celebrate
your commitment to excellence